EMPOWERED RELATIONSHIPS

An Introduction to Romantic Relationships

MARIA JESUS MARIN LOPEZ

BALBOA.
PRESS
A DIVISION OF HAY HOUSE

Balboa Press books may be ordered through booksellers or by contacting:

Balboa Press
A Division of Hay House
1663 Liberty Drive
Bloomington, IN 47403
www.balboapress.com
1 (877) 407-4847

Because of the dynamic nature of the Internet, any web addresses or links contained in this book may have changed since publication and may no longer be valid. The views expressed in this work are solely those of the author and do not necessarily reflect the views of the publisher, and the publisher hereby disclaims any responsibility for them.

The author of this book does not dispense medical advice or prescribe the use of any technique as a form of treatment for physical, emotional, or medical problems without the advice of a physician, either directly or indirectly. The intent of the author is only to offer information of a general nature to help you in your quest for emotional and spiritual well-being. In the event you use any of the information in this book for yourself, which is your constitutional right, the author and the publisher assume no responsibility for your actions.

Any people depicted in stock imagery provided by Thinkstock are models, and such images are being used for illustrative purposes only. Certain stock imagery © Thinkstock.

Print information available on the last page.

ISBN: 978-1-5043-4866-9 (sc)
ISBN: 978-1-5043-4867-6 (e)

Balboa Press rev. date: 01/14/2017

CONTENTS

ACKNOWLEDGMENTS

I would like to thank the many people who have made this book possible:

First and foremost, John, my beloved husband. I will be forever grateful for your continual unconditional love and support.

Keith Gaskin, for your patience and for believing in me. Thank you for the transcriptions.

Doreen Zeitvogel, you were sent to me and brought with you, your commitment, love and hard work. Thank you for editing my work.

All the clients and students, for your help in making this book possible.

All my friends and family, your love helps me to move forward.

'*My current understanding was born out of my own spiritual and healing journey. It is based on an accumulation of what I have learned through my studies and work, and it is emotionally grounded in the path that I walked from a superficially happy life to a spiritually, emotionally, mentally and physically full life. It has only been in recent years that I have found my true self – my inner contentment, continuity and peace.*'

Maria Jesus Marin Lopez

PREFACE

I had my first spiritual awakening at the age of six. I remember it very clearly. I was a very angry little girl. I felt unloved and misunderstood. I felt trapped in my body. I could feel the power of who I truly was, but I was the only one who could see this. Everyone else saw me as just a little girl – someone's little daughter. Then I moved to a new school, a Catholic school run by Salesian nuns. There was a little chapel beside my classroom, and one day I felt an inner calling to go in. As I walked in, I felt a warmth and calmness that allowed me to connect with my heart in a way I had never experienced before. From that moment, I knew everything would be OK – that I was loved and that my voice was heard. I knew that I wasn't alone, that I was part of something much greater. From that day something changed within me. My anger disappeared, and I knew that my life's purpose was to help others to reconnect with themselves.

Years later, I came to realize that 'helping others' brought me a lot of suffering. There was something that I was doing wrong. I couldn't understand why my life's purpose wasn't bringing me happiness. I then questioned myself: 'What do I need to do differently?' … and all I could hear, see and feel was the word 'empowerment'! At that stage in my life, the concept of empowerment was alien to me, but as I learned about it, I could see what I had been doing wrong. In helping others I had become trapped in doing everything for them, believing that I could take their suffering away from them; but now I knew that helping others meant to empower myself and lead by example. I understood that the way that I could truly help others would be by going deep within my own wounds and transcending the attachment to pain and illusion – by holding a non-judgmental sense of existence and open arms of infinite acceptance. When I transform my own suffering into love, I am enabling and supporting others to reconnect with their hearts. My belief changed from 'I'll do it for you' to 'If I can do it, so can *you*.' So whether your journey is decades or only days old, it is my deepest wish that this book will function as a transformational guide and impetus to further personal study and growth.

With much love to all,

Maria Jesus, March 2012

How It All Began

As we embark on this journey together, I would just like to say that I truly hope that this information will be life-changing or at least that it will bring some new ideas. We will be going a bit deeper into relationships which, for me, were a big question mark for a long time. I never really had a good model of what a good relationship was, and after many, many years, I copied my mother. By the age of thirty, I had had three major relationships – and they were just a disaster. I was completely heartbroken. I had a sense that I simply had lost myself. At the age of thirty, I said, 'I can't do this anymore – I give up. Relationships are just not for me.' I was really enjoying my career, my job … I had lovely friends. So I said, 'OK, well, I think this is enough … I'm happy with this. You know, I can just have an easy life.'

But one day, I was throwing away some old stuff, and I found a bunch of letters and journals that I used to write, so I started to read these journals. I had a journal of my first relationship, so I read that. Then, I found a journal of my second relationship … and I read that. And next, I came across a journal of my third relationship, so I read that as well. And I was shocked, because in every single relationship, what I wrote was the same. I *felt* the same. I still didn't know what to do with this information, even though I knew it meant something. At that point, I just didn't know what it meant. So after I reflected and really went inside myself, I realized that throughout my whole life, I had been blaming these men because *they* were making me feel this, and *they* were this and that, and I was 'poor me', a victim – I was a good person, a good girl ... how come all these things were happening to me? But what I realized was that what I said *they* were making me feel, *I* already had – feelings of being controlled, being rejected, being put down.

But then I realized that these feelings hadn't just started with my relationships. They had started many, many, many years ago in my family environment, in my relationship with my father, in the relationship between my father and my mother. So this was a big moment for me. I had this really important information – and that was great ... but now, I had to ask the question: 'OK, so, what do I do with this now?' In the meantime, though, something happened inside me, and I said, 'OK, I'll have one more relationship, and this one has to work. There's no way this relationship is going to fail – I'm just not going through that again. I'm going to do everything that I can to make this relationship work.' So with that intention in place – and it's well known that the Universe is quite good at responding to our intentions – the Universe brought me SOMEONE ... and you know what they say, you get what you ask for ... well, I got what I asked for. I had the opportunity to be in a relationship with a man where I could really explore and heal all of these wounds that I had. That might sound really nice, but it actually takes a lot of hard work and awareness and commitment to loving yourself in order to be in a loving relationship and to create that. What I realized was that in any given relationship – when we're talking about an empowered relationship – there is me (or you), and it is very important that we don't lose our identities; there are the other individuals in our lives, and it's very important that they don't lose their identities; and then there is the relationship, the energy that we both create together, which is a co-creation. And this is something I never knew about before … I never co-created in a relationship before. My style was that I would enter into a relationship and I would just lose myself. I had no sense of who I was – I would just completely lose myself to the other person.

So I learned that. I learned that the most important relationship any of us ever has is our relationship with ourselves. All our other relationships are nothing but a mirror that reflects how we view ourselves. Our relationships will be as positive or as negative as our view of our own selves.

Once I understood this, I realized that I had to relinquish my fears and live and love in the moment. The only person I could really pass judgment on was myself because it was only over myself that I had control. I could no more control the actions of others than I could fly to the proverbial moon.

Thus began my understanding of what it means to have empowered relationships and the amazing happiness that comes with the ability to have truly equal and loving relationships in life. I know firsthand that if you are willing to put in the time and effort to heal old wounds and scars and move past your current comfort zone, you too can have the joy and completeness that come with having empowered relationships in your life.

WHAT IS AN EMPOWERED RELATIONSHIP?

No one in this world can ever fulfill your needs – your need to be loved, your need to be supported, your need to be appreciated, your need to feel wanted ... The list is endless. Only you can fulfill these needs – only you can make yourself whole. Only then can you share who you are and move away from codependency and false expectations. Only then can you accept the love that is unconditionally offered instead of the love that is conditionally needed. And only then can you truly appreciate the opportunity to share love with someone else.

An Empowered Relationship is not a goal but a state of BEING, of becoming PRESENT for yourself, your partner and the world.

We spend our lives searching for LOVE, waiting for someone to love and someone to love us. When we meet that person, our hearts can open like never before, and sometimes we feel we would do anything for this other person and then expect the same in return.

But do we really know how to love? And most importantly, do we know how to be loved? Often, as soon as we open our hearts, strong feelings of fear can overtake us. Doubts and old wounds can show themselves, and we start to find excuses to move away from love.

For me, at this moment in time, the closet word for describing love is ACCEPTANCE.

The experiences we had as children formed our current view and relationship with love. We learned about love as we witnessed the relationship between our mother and father. That's where the journey started. Our parents, consciously and unconsciously, showed us the different dimensions of love.

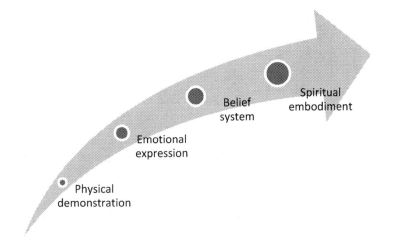

Spiritual embodiment

Belief system

Emotional expression

Physical demonstration

Love has many dimensions:

- Spiritual experience (embodiment of love, peace, communion with the Universe and All that is)
- Belief systems (do you believe you're lovable?)
- Emotional expression (joy, happiness, compassion)
- Physical demonstration (kissing, hugging, words, laughter)

Love means different things to different people.

Sometimes we just associate love with romantic love or parent/child love ... but love is experienced differently depending on our level of awareness. There is no right or wrong way to experience love – it depends on where we are in the 'love journey'. Our own understanding, feeling and embodiment of love might be different from the experience of others around us.

I find that love keeps showing different aspects of itself to me as I get older. I can now see how my relationship with love has evolved and will continue to grow and deepen.

It is a point I make that everyone shows love in their own unique way, and it is always good to accept that uniqueness.

The Shadow Side of Human Love

The shadow side of love can be overpowering, smothering, or overprotective. Too much love of a personal nature can turn into fear because that type of love and fear are the same energy. If you 'love too much', you're afraid to lose that love. This happens because we sometimes love selfishly. This can be seen with parents when they love their children so much and want the best for them but then smother them in the process, and their over protectiveness makes it difficult for the children to gain important survival skills. The parents are doing it out of love, but the shadow of that kind of love is not enough freedom. We have all done this ourselves as we all want to love and be loved in return.

A lot of times we expect people to love us the way we love. If I am 'touchy-feely', then I want others to be the same. Or if I am a 'doer', then I want people to do back for me. Unconsciously, I am saying, 'This is how I show love, and this is what I expect back.' With this frame of mind, I might accuse the people around me of not loving me because I don't accept or understand their unique way of showing love.

This has been one of the most important revelations of my life. When I drop my need to be loved in a specific way, which is limiting, I discover endless ways to experience love. Focus on how others are loving you instead of on how they are not!

The obstacles to love are always internal as whatever conflict is going on within is manifested externally.

Love doesn't come easy, but it can easily fly away. Our hearts are free, and in this freedom there is no possession, no attachment and no dependency.

- What do we fear the most?
  To lose our freedom.
- How can we lose our freedom?
  By giving our power away.
- How do we give our power away?
  When we live our lives through and for the other.

- How do we know when we are in our power?
  When we are centered in our hearts.

  The heart is the centre of our being. Our heart
  is strong, wise and loving. We need to learn to
  love compassionately, courageously and wisely.

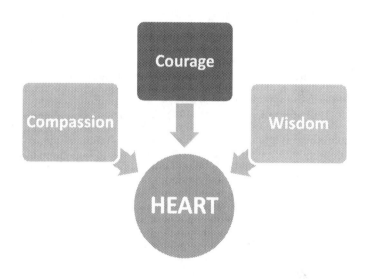

What Constitutes a Relationship?

The answer to this question would differ depending on who
you ask. The key word here is **'connection'**. When two or
more people are connected physically, emotionally, mentally or
spiritually, you could say that these people are in a relationship.
Depending on our personal backgrounds, we have all created
our own idea of what a relationship should look like. There
is nothing wrong with that, but problems can arise when
the people in the relationship have different views on what a
relationship is and what it can and should do for them.

The first mistake that a lot of us make is to believe that as soon as we leave the single life behind us, all our worries and problems will disappear as we enter into a relationship with the 'superhero' or 'super-heroine' that we have chosen as a partner. Suddenly, it becomes his or her duty to make us happy, to love us or to fulfill all of our needs. What we forget is that our partner, our loved one, has the exact same preconceived vision of the ideal relationship as we do – including the same dreams and expectations of us!

There is a possibility in any relationship that it may get to a place where it stops moving forward and becomes stuck. A relationship is like a dance. Every dance creates energy, and in a relationship, the dance involves three energies. There is you, your partner and the relationship. These are three different energies, and they don't always have to be linked to romantic involvement.

An empowered relationship is created by empowered individuals. To be empowered means that you are in complete acceptance of who you are. You can recognize the duality of who you are, and you can take ownership of your feelings, actions and beliefs. So the key concept is:

'Connection with Awareness'.

In an empowered relationship, *'I learn to love myself more through the experience of being with you'*. When we do this, we live in the moment and can take advantage of the endless possibilities that life has to offer.

THE HUMAN ENERGY FIELD

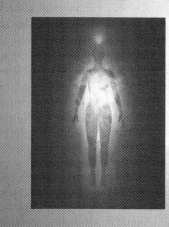

The Human Energy Field

- Physical Body
  Somatic sensations

- Emotional Body
  Feelings and emotions

- Mental Body
  Thoughts and beliefs

- Spiritual Body
  Karmic soul lessons

What Is Healing?

We are self-healing beings. Let's explore this a bit deeper and see how each body has its own intelligence.

- **Physical Body.** We all acknowledge that the body can and does heal itself given the chance. If you cut your finger, your physical body automatically releases plaques and antibodies to bring about self-healing. This is the Medical arena.
- **Emotional Body.** If your heart is broken by a loved one or a situation, your heart grieves, and grief is the natural emotion and first step in the healing process. It is only when grief is not acknowledged and allowed to simply be that we start erecting self-destructive walls that impede our life journey. This is the venue of Emotional Counselling.
- **Mental Body.** If you have allowed your mind to fill with toxic and negative thoughts, it is vital to your health and happiness to rid your mind and heart of this toxicity. You must acquire new learning skills and techniques to create a positive mindset. This is the arena of Psychotherapy and Cognitive Behavioural Therapy (CBT).
- **Spiritual Body.** Have you ever experienced a sense of isolation or disconnection from yourself, as though a part of you were missing? Welcome these times, as this is when your spiritual body creates situations that open the door to synchronization for reconnection! You need to be aware of the door opening and ready to walk through it. This is the venue of Spiritual Healing, allowing you to embody your true self.

What Is Energy?

Let's start with the concept that everything is ENERGY – energy being 'life force'. Everything we see, touch, feel and think is energy.

There is a principle that says that:

> **'Energy cannot be created or destroyed,**
> **it can only be transformed.'**

Energy vibrates – it moves at different speeds, or frequencies. The human energy field, also called the aura, is a magnetic field that surrounds our physical bodies. The physical body is at the lowest level of vibration, followed by the emotional, mental and spiritual bodies, the last of which is at the highest level of vibration. Any of these bodies is a gateway to the next. When they are all integrated, there is no separation so that we could even have a spiritual experience through the body.

Exercise:
From Negative to Positive

Let's take a minute to experience this right now.

Thoughts and feelings are forms of energy. If we have a negative thought, we can transform it into a positive one, and by doing that, we transform our experience.

So right now, take a deep breath and think of something negative ... Become aware of how you are feeling. What's happening in your body?

Now do the opposite. Think of something positive – something that makes you feel happy – and, again, become aware of what happens to your body ...

It's as simple as that. By transforming a negative thought into a positive one, we create the opposite experience. This can affect not only our bodies but our actual life circumstances and experiences as well.

What About the Spiritual Body?

It's in the spiritual body that we hold all the lessons we've learned as well as where we find our deep connection with All That Is. It's there, also, that we hold the wounds, the LACK of LOVE created by ourselves, our parents, our ancestors and, ultimately, humanity as a whole. This experience of a LACK of LOVE cannot be transformed with positive thinking alone. The energy we've created needs to be transformed with an equally powerful choice to go with the vibration, or energy, of

LOVE. The spiritual energy of LOVE creates loving thoughts which create loving feelings which create loving actions. If we look at love as only a feeling or a thought or an action, we won't be able to heal the spiritual wound.

Let's just imagine that when we first came into this world, when we were just little babies, we were 100% LOVE. As we grew older, someone may have told us, 'You are bad' or 'You are ugly', and suddenly that state of 100% LOVE changed to 80% LOVE with 20% LACK of LOVE. So life went on and things happened, and we kept changing our beliefs about ourselves until eventually we came to believe that we were only 40% LOVE and 60% LACK of LOVE.

That 60% that we don't love and accept about ourselves is what we call a **spiritual wound.**

That part of ourselves that we don't accept is what we can't accept in others, but when we judge someone else, we are really expressing self-judgment. If we only love ourselves 40%, that's all the love we are able to accept from others. Even if they love us at 70%, we can only connect with the same amount of love that we hold for ourselves.

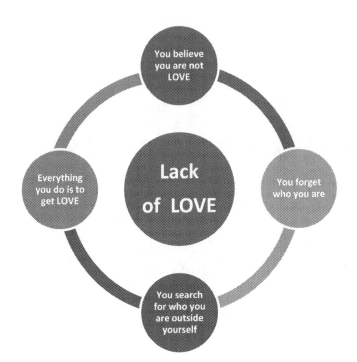

These spiritual wounds create thoughts. The thoughts create feelings and emotions. The emotions create a physical manifestation of the wound. That's why sometimes we can heal the way we think or our emotional state, but unless we look at the spiritual wound itself, that energy will still be active and play itself out in our lives. This wound then becomes a very powerful force in our lives until we can accept its existence, take responsibility for it, learn the lesson it's teaching us, make peace with ourselves and ultimately return to LOVE.

Healing the wound means that we choose to embark on the journey to once more become 100% LOVE.

THE DUALITY OF OUR EXISTENCE

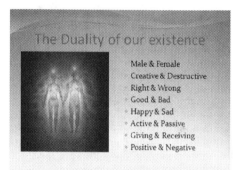

When we look at life as a duality, what happens is that we have to identify with one of the two polarities. Sometimes I say to people: *'The most dangerous thing you can do is to believe that you are a good person, because that means that the other person is bad'*, and sometimes a lot of the conflicts that we create in our lives come from holding on to one of these two polarities. *'I'm right';* therefore, the other person is wrong. *I'm a victim*; therefore, the other person is the perpetrator', and so on. When we identify ourselves with one polarity, we will create situations that will sustain that belief about ourselves, but often we will also see the other person as our counterpart.

I see these dualities as man-made and not Soul-made. Our minds have created this separation through black-and-white thinking, which in turn has created an experience of existence as a series of polarities.

Exercise:
Learning to Embrace Our Whole Being

So now, get a piece of paper and divide it into four columns.

In the first column, write a list of about twenty items that state something positive about yourself, for example, 'I am creative', 'I am intelligent' ...

In the second column, write another twenty items stating something negative, such as 'I am lazy', 'I am ugly'...

In the third column, write another twenty positive items, this time about people in general, such as 'People are nice', 'People are helpful' ...

And, finally, in the fourth column, write twenty negative items about people in general, such as 'People are rude', 'People are judgmental' ...

Now grab a red pen, and circle the equivalent opposites in Columns 1 and 2. For example, for 'I am stupid', you would also circle 'I am intelligent'.

Next grab a different color pen and do the same for Columns 3 and 4.

I am (Positive)	I am (Negative)	People are (Positive)	People are (Negative)
I am Intelligent	I am lazy	People are kind	People are rude
I am artistic	I am ugly	People are generous	People are
I am caring	I am loud	People are …	People are …
I am beautiful	I am stupid	peaceful	violent

What do you see? Do you have any conflicting identities? How, for example, can you believe yourself to be both stupid and intelligent at the same time?

The truth is that all of us hold both polarities within ourselves. Sometimes we **behave** stupidly, and at other times we behave intelligently. What we learn is that we are not our behaviour, our feelings or our thoughts but that we all have the potential to behave, think and feel however we choose. This process of choosing can be conscious or unconscious.

Beliefs are thoughts that we take to be true. So when we believe that we are 'intelligent' but we judge someone else as 'stupid', what that is telling us is that there is a part of ourselves that we don't accept. Only when we can learn to love the parts of ourselves that we judge as stupid or whatever the negative attribute might be can we truly find peace of mind. Being intelligent or stupid will no longer be an issue or something that we need to prove.

Emotions are energies experienced in the emotional body (anger, fear, love, joy, etc.). Feeling is the product of our relationship with the emotion, how we allow that energy (consciously or unconsciously) to flow and manifest through us. For example, when I feel anger, I might become violent whereas someone else might repress it or use that energy to speak up and take right action. Anger as an emotion is neither good nor bad, but how I relate to anger can be destructive or constructive. Emotions are signals, and it's useful to understand their meaning:

- Anger/Right action
- Sadness/Connection
- Powerlessness/Boundaries
- Guilt/Innocence
- Shame/Self-belief
- Fear/Love

When we try to avoid suffering, we are actually creating more of it. We find different ways to brush our feelings under the carpet until one day we trip over the pile. Instead, we need to identify what those feelings are trying to tell us.

When I feel sad, I feel alone, I feel unloved and I feel that nobody cares for me. I also feel that I cannot share myself. Sadness and isolation exist very close together. When I can listen to that sadness, I know that sadness is giving me a valuable gift. That sadness is giving me very important information. **Listen to your sadness with your Heart and not just with your Head!**

Meditation:
Sadness as your Teacher

Breathe into your heart now, and just listen to the beat of your heart.

Visualize your heart divided into two parts: a white part and a black part.

The white part holds love, happiness and joy.

The black part holds sadness, heartache and betrayal.

Now visualize the black part turning into a Teacher.

It can be male or female, and it holds the energy of a Higher Teacher. This is a very wise teacher, so ask him or her what he/she is trying to teach you.

Ask him/her about the purpose of your sadness.

Ask this teacher to show you how to deal with sadness in a more constructive way, so you can acknowledge the presence of sadness and learn whatever it is that you need to learn and then allow the sadness to move on.

It is just like the seasons. One season comes, and another one goes. That is the natural cycle of life.

Sadness comes, and sadness goes.

So allow yourself to make peace with sadness.

When we explore such energies as sadness and love, we need to understand that they are not separate. Anger and peace, fear and safety – these are two sides of one coin, part of the same dualistic reality. So sadness and love teach us the same thing but in different ways. It's like two different teachers teaching in two different ways but making the same point. Only when we can master both sadness and happiness can we find something in the middle that has nothing to do with sadness or happiness as we normally perceive them but is the marriage of both energies.

Can you love yourself when you are in the presence of sadness? YES!

Whenever you are feeling or thinking something negative, instead of repressing it or reacting to it, connect with it and understand what that feeling or thought is trying to communicate to you.

- **Spiritual imprint** – Soul lesson
- **Belief system** – A thought taken to be true
- **Emotion** – Emotional energy
- **Feeling** – Our relationship with the emotion
- **Action** – How we express, our behaviour

So if you are not your emotions, beliefs or behaviour, then who are you?

We could say that we are the collection of our life experiences, the things we've learnt, the fears we've faced and the service we've given. When I ask myself this question, I always connect strongly with the qualities of the Soul:

Wisdom

Truth & Healing

Will

Love

Peace

Freedom

Purity

In our life's journey, all the lessons that we need to learn evolve around these seven.

Meditation
Chakra Clearing with the Seven Crystals

As you inhale, really be aware of your breath ... and be grateful for your breath ... since it brings oxygen to your bloodstream ... and to your organs ... Sometimes we take breathing for granted ...

So as you're breathing, be aware of what is happening in your body ... whether there is tension anywhere ... If you feel tension, just allow your breath to calm the area ... and allow your gratitude for your breath to bring you a sense of relaxation ...

If your mind starts to wander ... that is OK ... just keep bringing your awareness back to your body ... Pick any area at all ... and just bring your awareness into your body and into that area ... Allow your mind to really be in your body ...

Be grateful for your feet ... How does it feel to have your feet on the ground ... inside your shoes ... Your feet take you places ... they do so much for you ...

Be grateful for your legs ... just connect with your legs ... just visualise all of the things they have done and the places they have taken you ... and connect with all the things that your legs can do ... like walking ... running ... kneeling ... dancing ...

Be grateful for your hands and your arms ... and connect with your hands and all the things that they do ...

Be grateful for your organs ... how they keep you alive ... Really acknowledge all of their functions ...

So really allow yourself to honour your body ... being aware of all the things that your body does ... consciously or subconsciously ... Really allow yourself to be present in your body ... to own your body ...

We are now going to connect with and tune ourselves to the Seven States of Being ... the True Identity of the Soul ...

The first state is Purity ... so just acknowledge and know that you are pure ... that your body is pure ... that it is the mirror of your soul ... Sometimes we judge our bodies as impure ... and sometimes society makes us feel bad about our bodies ... Sometimes we wish that we had no body ... or that we had a different body ... Sometimes, through different religions or different aspects of religion, we are told that our bodies are sinful ...

So allow yourself to remove all of those beliefs ... They don't belong to you ... they are just human judgements ... And allow yourself to connect with that part of you that is pure ... that part of you that is Pure Soul ... Know that Purity is not something that you can do or something that you can achieve ... Purity is what you are ...

So in your Root Chakra, at the base of your spine ... visualise a clear White Crystal radiating the energy of Purity ... and allow this vibration to transform any beliefs ... any emotions ... any spiritual imprints that do not match the vibration of Purity ... Just give yourself permission to release those and to truly embody the essence of your soul ... Your soul is pure ... your body is pure ...

Now bring your awareness to your Sacral Centre just below the belly button ... and visualise a Violet Crystal emanating the energy of Freedom ... Know that Freedom cannot be taken away from you or given to you ... since Freedom is who you are ... **Freedom is a state of being** ... it is the essence of your soul ... So ask yourself the question ... Are you allowing yourself to be free ... and if not ... how are you depriving yourself of Freedom ... We have grown up in a society that has made us believe that Freedom is outside ourselves ... and there is a part of us that still believes that Freedom is something that we have to fight for ... something that we need to look for ... But the truth is that Freedom lives within us ... So allow yourself to release any emotions or belief systems ... any spiritual imprints that move you away from being Freedom ... and as you allow those energies to transmute ... really connect with that part of yourself ... that essence of your Soul ... that knows that Freedom lies within you ...

Next bring your awareness to your Solar Plexus ... right where your stomach is ... and visualise a Ruby Crystal emanating the energy of Peace ... You are the source of Peace in your life ... When we disconnect ourselves from the true source of Peace ... we focus on the source of conflict ... and we feel attacked ... we feel the need to defend ourselves ... Somehow we lose touch with Peace ... but again, Peace is the essence of our Soul ... it is not something that we can achieve ... **Peace is a state of being** ... So allow yourself to connect with that part of yourself ...

Now bring your awareness to your Heart Centre ... right in the middle of your chest ... and visualise a Pink Crystal emanating the energy of Divine Love ... From a very early age we have learned to place the source of Love outside ourselves ... we have learned that if people like us or if people love us, then we are OK ... but if people reject us or if people don't like us ... that means that there is something wrong with us ... We judge ourselves based on what other people think or feel ... But Love cannot be given to us, and Love cannot be taken away from us ... since **Love is a state of being** ... Love is the essence of our Soul ... Love cannot be found outside ourselves ... it cannot be generated outside ourselves ... So allow the energy of the Pink Crystal to transmute any emotions ... any belief systems ... any spiritual imprints ... and allow them to be transformed ... allow yourself to be Love ...

Next bring your awareness to the Throat Centre ... and visualise a Sapphire Blue Crystal emanating the energy of Power ... This is the centre of communication ... In different societies, we judge communication in different ways ... In some cultures, we feel it is not our right to express who we are ... because other people might not like it and might find it offensive ... because other people might not agree with our expression of ourselves ... We feel ashamed to be who we are ...

But it is our divine right to be whoever we are ... to express whoever we are ... So again just allow those feelings of shame and judgement ... those emotions and belief systems ... those thoughts and spiritual imprints ... just allow them to be transformed ... knowing that it is your divine right to be who you are ... exactly as you are ...

Allow yourself to express your uniqueness ... for there is no one else like you ... You are unique ... and for that reason ... you are special ... **Power is a state of being** ... It cannot be given or taken away from you ... it is a quality of your Soul ...

Now bring your awareness to the Third Eye, which is located between your eyebrows ... and visualise an Emerald Green Crystal emanating the energies of Healing and Truth ... and allow the vibration of this Crystal to remove any veils of illusion ... of judgement ... of criticism ... of fear and false perception ... Allow yourself to see the world as it is ... to see the Truth in every situation ... allow yourself to bring Healing to yourself and to others ... because Truth and Healing are not things that you can get ... nor are they things that you can give ... **Truth and Healing are a state of being** ...

Now bring your awareness to your Crown Chakra right at the top of your head ... and visualise a Golden Yellow

Crystal emanating the energy of Wisdom ... Really allow yourself to connect with the Wisdom of your Soul ... to connect with that part of you that has all the answers ... that part of you that is connected to the Higher Wisdom ... and know that Wisdom cannot be given to you or taken away from you ... **Wisdom is a state of being** ...

So now that you have activated the Seven Crystals and the Seven States of Being ... know that you are Purity ... that you are Freedom ... that you are Peace ... and Love ... Power ... Truth ... and Wisdom ... Once you realise your true identity ... you can really be centred within yourself ... you know that you are the main provider of everything in your life ... that you don't need to go searching outside yourself for anything ... looking for anything ... since all the answers are inside of you ... You are Purity ... Peace ... Freedom ... Love ... Power ... Truth ... and Wisdom ...

So now ... very gently ... return ... move your toes ... give yourself a good stretch ... and when you're ready ... open your eyes ...

Connecting with Our True Essence

Sometimes we create a false sense of identity like 'I am my job' or 'I am a mother' or 'I am this and I am that'; but we create this sense of identity from something that we do. If I work at something, it's just something that I do – it does not make me who I am. There can be a lot of who I am in what I do, but it's separate from my essential identity.

The true essence of our identity comes from connecting with the Seven States of Being. A lot of the situations that we create in our lives probably centre around a lack of love or a lack of freedom or peace. The reason these situations happen is that we are really trying to connect with that part of ourselves, so we create many situations in our lives that teach us how to have peace or how to have freedom. Once we realise that this is what we are doing, then we can start to be masters of our lives, and we can start to see that the major situations we create don't just happen out of the blue. There may be a pattern in our lives where we feel controlled all the time, and we may feel that we're victims of this pattern because it's always about control, control, control. But if we look at this kind of thing from a place of, 'OK, so this sense of being controlled means that I am not free; therefore, what I am looking for is a sense of freedom;' if we look at it from this point of view and we take control of the pattern and our own search for freedom, then we can begin to understand what is going on in our lives. We can become more aware of the lack of freedom and the lack of love as the purpose in our experiencing these lessons. So if you are searching for peace and this is something that you really want in your life because you feel you don't have it, that just means that you are not connected to it, and that's why you are trying to find peace to begin with. If there is conflict in your life and you feel no peace, ask yourself how you can create peace in those situations. A peaceful situation is not going to appear out of the blue, because peace needs to be created. Once you realise this, you will see that peace is not something that you can give or take but that the energy of peace is something that you are and that you embody.

When we look around, we see that some people are always in a financial crisis or a relationship crisis, or they isolate themselves. Individuals create many different situations for themselves. They create these situations because somehow, at some point, they have become disconnected from the essence of who they are. They feel that love is outside of them and, therefore, that nobody loves them and nobody will ever love them. But love comes from within. Sometimes they wait for someone to come along and show them how to be free. But freedom comes from within, and no one else can help them to be free. No one is going to say, 'OK, you're free to be who you are.' Only we can create the freedom we need. Even if someone were to tell us that and if that person were a free person, our own freedom could still only come from inside of us.

When there is a recurring theme in our lives, that means that we are not integrating whatever aspect of ourselves is needed to deal with that issue. Once we integrate that part of ourselves, the pattern stops. Then we have that part of the puzzle, and we can move on to the next one. We all have recurring themes in our lives, and when we manage to solve them, it is because we have empowered ourselves and said that we've had enough. In doing so, we become strong, and we change the pattern. The first step is to recognise that we don't want the specific pattern in our lives. Then, when we find the determination and intention to say, 'No more – this ends now', that's when real change happens.

THE EMPOWERED 'I'

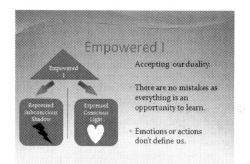

The empowered **'I'** means that I am in complete acceptance of who I am – of both the energies that I accept and the ones that I repress, namely, my light and my shadow, my conscious and my unconscious being. I am aware of the parts of myself that I repress – the parts that are subconscious or in the shadow – when I can identify what they are playing out and what it is they are telling me about myself. This is the great thing about relationships: we cannot hide from our subconscious or the things that we repress because in a relationship, the other person is the mirror of everything that we repress, whether that means our gifts or our faults.

When we look at ourselves from a place of empowerment, there are no mistakes. We cannot do right, and we cannot do wrong. We cannot be bad, and we cannot be good. When we look at ourselves from an empowered place, everything that we do is just an opportunity for us to learn to love ourselves more. It's an opportunity for us to know ourselves better. The result is that a lot of the power struggle disappears within ourselves and with others. Sometimes when we say, 'I am an angry person', 'I am a good person' or 'I am a happy person' and 'he is a selfish person' or a 'generous person', we are actually identifying how we feel at that moment, and we are stating who and what we are.

As we move about in our daily lives, we usually only show people those parts of ourselves that we accept. So when we meet someone, and especially when we start a romantic relationship, at first everything is amazing. He or she is so lovely and nice, and *'he is the one'*, or *'she is the one'*. This is the honeymoon period, as we all know so well. Then something happens, and the unseen part shows up, and this is often the beginning of conflict.

Now in a traditional relationship, there is no boundary. Usually, in these types of relationships, the individuals are linked – they function as a unit. There is no sense of individual identity, so if he wants to go to the pub, she has to go along. If she wants to go shopping for three hours on a Saturday, he has to go along. They see themselves as being together, and if they don't do everything together, there will be repercussions later on. This is what happens in the disempowered style of relationship where there is a lot of co-dependency. His job is to fulfil her needs, and her job is to fulfil his needs. His job is to love her, and her job is to love him. Giving and receiving is great, but when we believe that our identity and source of love lie with the other person, we lose touch with the real source of both identity and love.

5

THE MIDDLE "WE"

The Middle "WE"

- Empowered I is when I accept all that I am

- WE is co-created by I + I

- WE is the place where I learns to love and accept all aspects of self

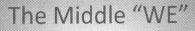

The Empowered 'I' is when I accept all that I am.

'WE' is co-created by 'I' plus 'I'.

'WE' is the place where the 'I' learns to love and accept all aspects of SELF.

When we are in an Empowered Relationship, the whole dynamic changes:

The participants in the relationship hold before them the Empowered 'I', which includes:

1. the things that they accept about themselves and
2. the things that they repress about themselves.

Both 'I's provide the relationship energy, and in the middle is the 'WE' which is created by both, and this is where communication happens. I know this might sound a bit cold and not very romantic, but in reality it is a contract between two people. When you go for a job interview, they ask you lots of questions, and when you sign your contract, you know exactly what your job is. There is no difference in a relationship. In a sense, both people are signing an unwritten contract, and each contract will be different for every two people who form a relationship.

So in our example here we find ourselves witnessing the energy of a relationship that is being co-created. We have Ana, a beautiful individual, and Tony, another beautiful individual, and they have chosen to come together to co-create something. Tony will hold space for Ana when she is having a bad time so that she can heal and vice versa. So it's teamwork. In an empowered relationship, there is no projection and there is no blame. Whatever is going on with Ana belongs to Ana, and whatever is going on with Tony belongs to Tony. When there is a conflict, there will be one person who expresses it actively while the other person acts it out passively.

Respect as Acknowledgement and Acceptance

When we are respected, we feel that we are accepted and listened to. It is the opposite of the dismissiveness we experience as children because people think, 'You're only a child. What would you have to say?' This is actually a dismissal of another human being, which means that he or she is not being listened to and that we don't accept whatever that child needs to say. We are all looking for the attention and respect that shows the world, 'OK, I am here and I am holding my space, so acknowledge me ...' That's why kids sometimes misbehave. They learn that when they misbehave, they get attention. They then continue to misbehave because they need this attention, but this just reinforces the misbehaviour.

Respect is about acknowledging the other person. This is a definition that works very well for me. Like a lot of people, I had no clue as to what self-respect was because I never had it. Now, when I am in a situation where someone is projecting anger onto me for no reason, what works for me is to say, 'OK, I can see and I acknowledge that you are angry.' That way, I give them respect by acknowledging that the person's anger exists and that that is fine. BUT – and this is where self-respect comes in – even though I respect where that person is, it is not OK to project that anger onto me. The other person's line is there, and my line is here. I am here for other people, but I will not take on their anger. It all comes down to how we use our anger and whether we express it in a constructive way. It is OK to be angry and to express it, but don't project it onto me or someone else, because I will not tolerate disrespect, and they shouldn't, either. So that is an instance of how we can lead by example by accepting and understanding what's going on in another person's space.

Holding Space for Each Other

When one person experiences pain, the other person will hold space, allowing the first person to heal through his or her acceptance. I find that whatever I implement I have to do for myself first. Also, in cases where the other person has a resistance to it, I hold space for myself first. When I hold the energy for myself, usually what happens is a transformation in the other person. Of course, there is no guarantee because we all have free will. But usually, if I establish love, respect and confidence, and if I then send it to the other person as a vibration, there is a good chance that the other person will pick it up and that we will establish a common ground.

Holding space allows the other person to just be. If our partners have a meltdown, they are showing us a part of themselves that is wounded and unloved. So when we hold space for them, we are allowing them to love and respect themselves more. When we feel that we are nothing without the other person, that is co-dependency, and it can take many forms. To be empowered is to be in your own energy, because the true source of love, freedom and power lies within us. I'm not saying that we are completely independent people and that we don't need to interact with anyone, but it's also important to see that it's not a case of one person having a problem that needs to be fixed by someone else.

Relationships should be a place where we feel safe. We shouldn't feel that we need to be perfect all the time because in reality we are not. We are human beings with different emotions. We also have different seasons in our lives. A lot of times, we demonstrate a lot of talent and want to do many things, and then there are other times when we want to do nothing more than just sit around and watch movies – and that's also OK. When we are in an empowered relationship, it's about being ourselves, respecting ourselves and having boundaries, and just allowing each person to grow within the relationship.

So the aim of the relationship here is that Tony can learn to love himself through being with Ana and that Ana can learn to love herself through being with Tony. It's not so much about Ana loving Tony and Tony loving Ana but about both of them sharing love. We all need to experience both polarities of giving love and receiving love so that we can learn to embody love in its totality. When we feel that we are not being loved enough, then we need to learn from both polarities – the giving and the receiving polarity. They are different extremes, and our goal is to get to the middle point where we can embody and be love.

It's also about allowing for individuality. For example, metaphorically speaking, Tony can really enjoy being a Manchester United fan, and Ana can be a Liverpool follower. When they know this and when they reach a place in the middle where they accept and respect this, then they will find a different way of experiencing life. Establishing self-respect is the key to having others respect you, which is a very important lesson I had to learn. Growing up with my family, I didn't know what respect was, and consequently I found myself in relationships where I was very disrespected and didn't know that I was being disrespected. I thought that was just the way it was. Then I learned that that wasn't the case, but I also learned from my relationships that we generated disrespect together because I didn't respect myself to begin with. We co-created the experience from our own internal experience. Everything that happens within both individuals is co-created. So as I said before, there is the basic energy which one person acts out actively while the other one acts it out passively. One is the giver, and the other is the receiver. It's just sometimes easier to blame the active ones as the bad ones because their role is more obvious. But if you happen to be in the middle of a struggle, ask yourself what you're contributing with your 50%. What part are you playing in co-creating your experience? Because I guarantee that the person that is disrespecting you might not be disrespecting your friend.

Boundaries

We cannot control another person's behaviour. What we can control is our reaction to other people's behaviour.

In my experience, there are three types of boundaries: no boundary, the wall and the empowered boundary.

- When we have **no boundary**, there is no separation between other people's feelings and thoughts and our own. This can affect us in many ways: physically, emotionally, mentally and/or spiritually. When we have no boundary, somehow we become a magnet for negativity.

- When we use **the wall boundary**, we isolate ourselves as a way to protect ourselves. We put ourselves in a box or behind a wall. It is true that we keep negativity away, but we also keep love away. With this boundary, we can't feel anything from the outside.

- When we use **the boundary of empowerment**, we are in a place of self-love and self-acceptance. Therefore, we don't become attached to negativity, and we connect with the true essence of our being as 'Pure Love'. When we empower ourselves, our presence can empower others.

Exercise:
Creating a Boundary of Empowerment

Visualize a golden energy ball between your heart and your stomach.

This golden energy radiates Self-Love and Self-Acceptance.

Now allow this golden energy to expand until you are surrounded by it, like you are inside a golden egg.

Become aware of how you feel when you are inside this boundary of empowerment that radiates Self-Love and Self-Acceptance.

"I am Self-Love, Self-Acceptance and Self-Respect"

People tend to treat us the same way we treat ourselves.

If you love and respect yourself, others will love and respect you, too.

Co-Creation

The first thing that I look at is myself, and the second is the area of co-creation. Sometimes I feel that we make the mistake of stopping with the first step, where we see our own self as the creator of absolutely everything in our lives. If we believe this when dealing with other people, then we are not acknowledging their creativity. We can create everything that has just to do with us, and we have the power to change the things around us, but when we have a relationship with someone else, it's a fifty-fifty co-creative process.

So when talking about empowered relationships, I am really referring to co-creation. When I can create the life that I want not only for myself but in my dealings with others, then I am co-creating with them. The first thing to do is to make the commitment to ourselves to be responsible for our half of the energy created in every single relationship that we have. We need to move away from the belief that we are powerless as well as from the belief that we can control every single aspect of what goes on between us and other people. Again, our goal should be to find that fifty-fifty balance which is the place of true union.

Male and Female Energies

The left side of the brain holds the male energy, and the right side holds the female. As we can see in this world, especially today, there are a lot of women with very strong male energy, and there are a lot of men with very strong female energy. This has nothing to do with sexual orientation because sexual energy is a different thing.

- **What are some of the qualities generally associated with male energy?**
  Focus, Drive, Power, Action, Strength, Decisiveness, Impatience
- **What are some of the qualities associated with female energy?**
  Sensitivity, Emotionality, Nurturing tendencies, Passion, Understanding, Caring, Thoughtfulness, Passivity, Receptivity

Accepting and Balancing Both Energies

All of us have experienced these qualities personally, so this tells us that we all hold both male and female energies regardless of whether we have a male or female body. Every single human being in this world has both energies. Whether we emphasize one or the other depends largely on our environment and training. If you are a girl, for example, having certain qualities may not be safe, or it may be considered inferior or not good in some way. If you are in a family with all brothers, you may feel that you are different and therefore that there is something wrong with being a girl. When this is the scenario, the girl may repress her female energy and only want to emphasize her male energy. She will try to copy the males because she feels that they are better. Another scenario that can occur is when a girl is spoiled and the people around her either never demand anything from her or don't let her do anything. In a case like that, she will only use her female energy and will suppress her male energy.

She feels that if she really uses her female energy that she will be looked after and taken care of like a little princess. As a result, she does not want to know anything about her male energy because she thinks that if she brings it out in her behaviour, men won't like her. So here are two different scenarios where one girl suppresses her male energy while another suppresses her female energy. Exactly the same thing can happen with men, and this is our challenge when we come into this world.

In my own life, I have had more experience repressing my female energy and emphasizing my male energy because it feels safer in this world. It depends on what environment I am in. I sometimes ask myself, 'Am I really using my female energy as I feel that I'm manifesting more male energy?' Or if I'm in a different place: 'Am I really utilising my male energy?' If I'm in a place that is more nurturing, I find that I use much more of my female energy.

When we talk about bringing out both our male and female sides, what that means is being both focused, active and warrior-like and, at the same time, being nurturing, intuitive and receptive. This is what it means to be in a state of balance, when we can actually be happy being both at the same time, knowing that we have both energies and that we don't need to repress either side of ourselves just because we are a man or a woman.

> • **What is your Inner Female like?**
>   **What qualities does she have?**
>
> • **What is your Inner Male like?**
>   **What qualities does he have?**

Maintaining an Open Line of Communication Between the Inner Male and Female

If you are experiencing communication problems in your relationship, it would be good to get your Inner Male and Inner Female talking to each other. It's very important, now that you are aware of it, to keep that union going. Allow your Male and Female to communicate with each other in order to find out what they each need and want. If you find yourself trying to fill a need from outside, then stop yourself and say, 'This is not right. I have to provide this for myself. Either my Inner Male or my Inner Female needs to provide this for me – I cannot get it from outside myself.'

Exercise: Write to your Inner-Male & Inner-Female

If you have time and feel like writing a little letter to your Inner Male or Inner Female, then do it to explore the issue a bit more. You may be amazed at what comes up. Ask yourself what you need. This is whatever you're projecting outwards, and usually you will want other people to support you. That's the old way of doing things. The way from now on is to ask yourself, 'How can I support myself in what I am doing?'

Check with your heart. Find a way to provide that communication between your Male and your Female. Allow them to have a conversation. Writing it down will get it out of your system.

Meeting in the Middle

The longing we have in our lives to meet our counterpart in another man or woman is about making the invisible part of ourselves visible – we are searching for the union of our inner male and inner female outside of ourselves. This is the part of our journey where we look for a partner, or 'the One'. But 'the One' is within us. The mirror in the form of the visual man or woman we have outside ourselves is not separate from the one we have within ourselves. As we move forward in our lives and evolve as souls, our partners grow with us – or if they don't grow with us, someone else will come along, and the visual part of ourselves will grow together with that person.

When we are aware of this concept of inner and outer energy forms, then we understand that there is the part of ourselves that is the visible part, the part of ourselves that is invisible, and a third energy that is created in the middle, which is the energy of the relationship between those two parts. If, for example, I'm in a relationship with a man, I have my male and female energies and the middle energy that they create; he has his male and female energies along with the middle energy that they create; and we then both create another middle energy between the two of us, which is the relationship.

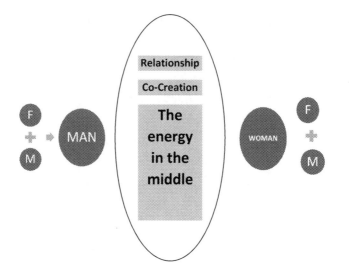

The key to a harmonious relationship, whether internal or external, is to communicate through the energy in the middle. The energy in the middle is where both aspects of the self and partner unite, whether we are dealing with a partner outside of our physical selves or with our own inner issues. So, for example, instead of saying 'I need you to be nicer to me', if I bring that energy to the middle and see what's happening there, it functions like a council where we can meet and talk. We can then see the real issue that is blocking our mutual support.

Everything that we bring to the middle affects the other person. When we are in a relationship, this is how things change and shift. So if there is something you are not happy about, you can go to the energy of the middle through meditation and have an inner talk about it. Then, when you meet with your physical partner later on, the issue often gets solved then and there. I have proven this, and it is amazing. There is no need for 'You did this, and you said that' or 'I need this, and I need that.' You fix things in the middle. It's so incredibly powerful that sometimes it can be really scary to ask how an issue can be solved just by energetically sitting around a visualized table talking about it and then seeing the problem solved in real life by communicating through the middle energy.

Again, if your partner holds a lot of anger, for example, the anger that he or she holds is automatically brought to the middle. If you or the other person is not aware of this middle energy, then if the anger is projected onto you, you may not know where it's coming from. This anger is not being directed at you – it's just anger that this person holds; but because there is no middle boundary, the anger comes towards you, and whatever you contribute to the relationship goes directly to the other person as well. When we become aware of the energy in the middle, then the anger that either one of us holds goes to the middle. That makes it possible for the other person to ask, 'OK, what is this about? Does this have to do with me? or is this your own issue?' So keep your subjective views in the middle. You can then have a dialogue, fix what is happening right there and then see the effect in your lives because of it.

The great thing is that, although we can do this together, until we reach that point, one person can do it without help from the other. We do not need to have the other person present. Whether we work consciously or unconsciously, this middle energy is happening anyway because that is how we are linked. This doesn't just apply to romantic relationships – every relationship has a middle ground.

I am sure you are also aware that there is often one person in a relationship that makes the decisions. What that person says goes – we have all witnessed this. When one person tries to control everything, the energy that should be in the centre will not be there to the same extent because the two original energies will not be balanced. When we have no boundaries, our problems become too close to us, and we feel that all these problems are our own and that we have to fix everything. In a case like that, the other person might feel that he or she doesn't have a say in the relationship because we are bringing in that kind of controlling energy. With healthy boundaries, there should always be three distinct energies; so if you see two people communicating through the energy in the middle and one of those people is attempting to control the relationship, just have a sense of where that energy is. What is happening to that middle energy? The important thing is to allow the energy of the middle to really function in the middle and to communicate with each other through this middle ground.

If I transmit a judgement such as 'women are lazy' to the middle, and the other person similarly sends her energy where her energy is not in truth, when the energy comes into the middle, that's when healing happens. The judgement is healed because I no longer hold it. As a result, my relationship with her changes. So it's about both of us becoming aware of the feelings and thoughts that we are projecting onto each other, whether they're positive or negative – things like 'He is like that' and 'She is like that', etc. If we bring all our judgements to the middle, then we won't hold anything negative towards the other person, and both people will be free of each others' projections. This is how we can solve things without blaming each other, and this is how real healing happens between two people – when they bring their issues to the middle without targeting each others' hopes and fears.

Your partner is there to help you get through whatever lesson you're learning at the moment. It might not be in a loving way – it might be more forceful. But the important thing is to be aware that the energy in the middle is created in every relationship that we have, since that is how we communicate with each other.

Exercise for Two
Projecting into the Middle

Sit or stand facing each other ...

Close your eyes ... and go to that place deep within yourself ...

Now really bring back all of those memories and all of those times when people told you that you were stupid ... bring back all of those situations when you called yourself stupid or someone else made you feel stupid ... remember all the judgements that you made about yourself being stupid ... and project all of those feelings onto the person in front of you ...

Become aware of when you are projecting the energy of being stupid ... and be aware of what you are receiving as well ... Really bring back all of those people and situations when you felt stupid or you were made to feel stupid and all the connotations that are attached to that energy, and be aware of how you feel ... Become aware of the energy and space between the two of you ... Keep the projection going...

Now have a clear sense of yourself and the energy in the centre as well as the other person's energy ... There are three entities ... three energies ... three spaces ... so the two of you are going to project the energy of being stupid into the middle ... not towards each other anymore ... just into the middle ... Be aware of the energy in the middle ... how do you feel now that this projection is not how do you feel now that this projection is not being focused towards you? ... It no longer goes straight to the other person ...

Now allow yourselves to become empowered ... Go to that place between your heart and your solar plexus ... and visualise and expand that Golden Energy of Empowerment ... Really feel empowered ... feel grounded ... centred ... and connected ... Really become aware of your own space of Empowerment ... also really become aware of the other person's space of Empowerment ...

Now become aware of the energy in the middle ... and from that place of Empowerment ... bring yourself to the middle to heal the space between the two of you ... You are going to have a conversation with the other person in the middle ... so hold the intention to accept and respect yourself and the other person ... and allow the energy to do its work ... Just be empowered ... and allow the energy in the middle to become an energy of Peace ... Harmony ... Acceptance ... and Love ...

When you are in that place ... become aware that it doesn't really matter who is stupid ... or who is intelligent ... because in that place ... you can accept that part of you that is stupid ... just as you can accept that part of you that is intelligent ... and because of that ... you can accept the part of the other person that is stupid ... and the part that is intelligent ... It doesn't really matter ... because from this space in the middle you can really accept the other person as who they are ... as an empowered being that is on a journey of self-discovery and self-evolution ... just the same as you ... You realise that there is no separation ... between you and the other person ... because you know that as souls ... both of you have to learn the same lessons ... both of you have the same challenges ... both of you have the same aspirations ... both of you are One ... So now ... in your own time ... with this new sense of yourself and others ... slowly come back ... very slowly ... very gently ... open your eyes ...

Identifying the Games

Once you change your focus to the middle, issues are easy to dissolve because you are not identifying your pain with the other person. Now when someone comes to me and they are a bit angry, I know that it has nothing to do with me. If I take something as a personal attack, then I have to defend myself since this is one of the emotional games that we play a lot of the time. But if someone comes to me and says, 'Blah blah blah,' and I don't take offence at it, then it is not an attack. What's important is that you can identify what game is being played and what issues are being triggered in you.

Every situation is different, and it's good to identify what game you are playing with each person. Ask yourself, 'Am I always playing the victim with this person? or am I playing the stupid person ... or am I always being a bitch with this person?' It's not always about the other person − it's often about us. So if you're feeling like a victim with someone, then try to discover what message that victim feeling is giving you. The message may be that your boundaries are not strong enough; so in that case, you need to form stronger boundaries. If someone is making you feel attacked all the time so that you feel that you have to defend yourself, then try to find out how you're giving your power away when you should be saying 'This is my space, and this is who I am – and I don't have to justify who I am.' There is a message in all the things that we feel. It's great to feel sadness, but what is that sadness telling us so that we can better ourselves? It's great to feel anger, but what is the anger trying to say to us? What is the message of the emotion? The energy that you send out is perceived by the other person, so if energetically you are still feeling the wound of the four-year old when you talk with your boss, then you can talk to him all you want, but you are still that four-year old. You need to bring yourself to the point of being an adult energetically so that you can then communicate with the energy of an adult and not the energy of a four-year old. That's the difference that is needed so that whatever game is being played won't be played anymore.

So it's about energetically changing yourself so that you can face the world. Like attracts like, so if you are still rooted in the old energy, then you will receive the same thing into your experience. Also, if you want to create harmony with someone, then ask yourself about the intention of that desire for harmony. Is it because you don't like confrontation, or do you just want to be liked? You don't need to be in harmony with everyone, although a lot of us feel guilty if we are not in harmony with every single creature in the world and we have difficulty being in their presence. We need to understand that that's OK. You cannot be friends with everyone in the world. What works for me is to first work at it energetically – to change myself and then confront the issue from this new place. That is much easier and faster.

When you are empowered and you know who you are as a soul, if whatever I say to you doesn't ring true, then it simply cannot affect you. Only what you believe to be true can affect you. So if you believe that you are stupid or bitchy, then that projection will penetrate because you believe it to be true, and this will hurt you. If you don't hold that energy or belief, it won't do anything to you.

Exercise:
Individual Projection

Close your eyes ... and go to that deep place within your heart ... Allow yourself to breathe ... nice and deep within your heart ... allow your heart to open ... Allow yourself to be in that place of empowerment ... that place where you know who you are ... that place where you have access to your whole soul ... that place where you feel grounded ... centred ... and connected ...

Now visualise in front of you the person you have chosen ... See them as they truly are ... as an empowered being ... just like you ... See them growing and evolving and learning about themselves ... And visualise between the two of you ... the third energy ... the energy in the middle ...

Now bring your issue there ... whatever the conflict is ... whatever the discord ... just bring it there ... If you have had an argument ... you can bring it to that space ... or whatever is specifically bothering you ... bring it to the middle ... This energy in the middle ... is the energy of Acceptance ... of Peace ... of Harmony ... of Freedom ... and Love ... So surround the conflict with those energies ... It is here in the middle where you can both come to an understanding ... it is here in the middle where you can express your needs ...

So allow the other person to express his or her needs ... and when you have both expressed your own needs ... you will both know ... that it's not the other person's job to fulfil your needs ... you both know that you are responsible for fulfilling your own needs ... that you are responsible for providing Love for yourself ... that you are responsible for providing Freedom for yourself ... that you are responsible for giving support to yourself ...

So in this place in the middle ... both of you now take responsibility for your own lives ... your own happiness ... Just feel the energy of that ... Energetically you have found harmony ... energetically you have a greater sense of understanding and acceptance ... energetically you are taking ownership of your own feelings and thoughts ... and so is the other person ...

So holding that energy that is between the two of you ... that energy of Peace ... of Harmony ... of Acceptance ... of Freedom ... and Love ... really look into the eyes of the person in front of you ... and see them as an empowered being ... See yourself being grateful to them for showing you your deepest wounds ... and be grateful that they are enabling you to become more of who you are ... They are giving you a clue as to what it is that you need to look at deep within yourself ... Also feel the gratitude coming from them ... since the two of you are of service to each other ...

Now ... still retaining this sense of Gratitude ... and Peace ... very slowly ... and very gently ... bring yourself back ... and open your eyes ...

THE FOUR MAJOR WOUNDS

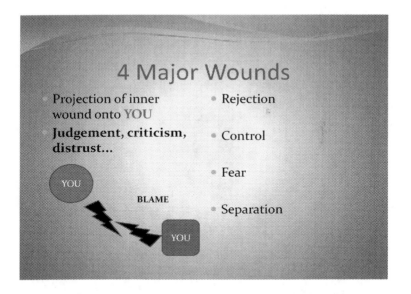

We are going to focus on what I call the four major wounds that we all have and experience in our relationships. For each of us, there are patterns that we just keep repeating and repeating over and over again, and when our wound really shows up, the Empowered 'I' disappears and becomes 'You'. All of a sudden, it's not about Tony any more – it's about Ana, and vice versa. He is no longer enough. He doesn't wash the dishes or whatever, and she is not doing this and that. This is how the Empowered 'I' disappears and becomes 'You' as we project outside of ourselves. When we project, it usually means that we blame others and put them down through criticism as we judge all the polarities mentioned earlier.

We all have many defense mechanisms. These defense mechanisms are an unconscious process created by us as a way to protect ourselves from experiencing emotional and/or mental pain. When we become aware of these in our relationships, we see the other person under a different light. The most common defense mechanisms are:

- **Projection** – The act of projecting or the state of being projected upon. When we project onto others, we are seeing our own hidden traits, emotions and beliefs projected as a result of the belief that those feelings originate in others instead of ourselves.
- **Denial** – The act of denying painful thoughts as though they don't exist.
- **Repression** – The attempt to protect ourselves from impulses or ideas that would otherwise cause anxiety if they were to become conscious.

Have a look at your own relationship and ask yourself the following questions:

- What aspects of myself am I projecting onto my partner?
- What thoughts and feelings am I denying in myself?
- Which impulses am I repressing in my relationship?

Try to do the exercise below and see what projections come up.

What I judge and criticise in my partner is a projection of ME	
I project onto YOU ...	I own my projection ...
When I have a bad day at work, I come home and get mad at you	When I'm angry, I have no right to pass it on to you. If I have had a bad day at work I can let you know that, although I might need a few moments alone to disconnect from work so that I can be really present with you.

Also try to identify the projections your partner has towards you.

It's a good idea to have a conversation with ourselves so that we don't pick a fight with the person who happens to be the target of our anger. It amazes me how, when I solve an issue within myself, I also resolve it in my relationships. A lot of this has to do with projection so that if I remove the inner issue, then the other person cannot react because there is no energy to feed the reaction. It would be like playing a ping pong game and suddenly having no ball. When we play the ping pong game of I project-you project-I project-you project, then we are at it all the time. But if we remove our projections, even if the other person hits the ball, it just goes over the net, and there is no game. It's all about knowing that this process of mutual projection is a game and that we can choose to play or not to play. This ping pong game is going on within us all the time, and that is then mirrored on the outside.

THE WOUND OF REJECTION & ABANDONMENT

Unconscious spiritual lesson

- When the wound of Rejection and Abandonment is active, we attract the person that abandons us or the one that we abandon

Beliefs of rejection and abandonment

- He/she will leave
- There's no point in loving all the way as this will end
- I'll break it off before he/she does
- I'm all alone – no one loves me

Feelings of rejection and abandonment

- Lack of self-worth
- Loneliness
- Broken heartedness
- Disconnection from one's heart

Abandonment behaviour

- Giving someone up
- Withdrawing one's support or help
- Leaving completely and finally
- Pushing someone away

In this case, Tony is rejecting Ana, and Ana is being rejected, but the energetic wound will be the same for both. Therefore, there is no sense that because he's doing the rejecting, he is the bad one. Both hold the same wound, and together they are co-creating rejection and abandonment.

Energetically, in this relationship, Tony is rejecting Ana and Ana is being rejected. His energy is pushing her, and she is pulling back.

What do you think Tony is thinking and feeling as he rejects Ana?

What do you think Ana is feeling as she is being rejected?

Think back on your life.

Have you ever been in Tony's position, or have you ever been in Ana's position?

All of us have the potential within ourselves to reject and be rejected because the essential wound is the energy of rejection. Sometimes we express that wound actively when we reject another person or group of people, and sometimes we express it passively when we are rejected.

What happens when Ana tries to interact with Tony?

If she tries to approach him, he resists.

This is where a lot of people get stuck.

What happens if Tony starts running away?

Ana will run after him.

How many times have we been in this situation?

Oh, yeah – 'I sent him a text message and he hasn't replied, so I'll text him again', or 'maybe he didn't get that text, so I'll send him another one just in case.' Or 'maybe the weather messed up the last one', or 'I'll send him another text just to let him know that I am never going to text him again.'

The energy that this creates is that he is being chased, so, obviously, he is going to run. Now somebody here has to stop running at some point, so if Ana stops running, then Tony will probably stop running because she is no longer chasing him, so where would he go? At some point, Ana says, 'OK, I am going to hold my space, and I am not going to go outside myself so that I'm chasing someone else for love. I am just going to wait.' Now every story is different, but there is a good chance that

Tony will think differently at that point and start wondering how Ana is doing.

When we hold the energy of rejection within ourselves, we are essentially rejecting ourselves. On a deeper level, it is not even so much that we are rejecting ourselves as that we are rejecting love. In Tony's case, Ana represented the source of love for him, so as he got scared of love, he started pushing her away because he was actually pushing love away. In an empowered relationship, when Tony accepts his wound of rejection and Ana accepts her rejection and they are both able to experience this through the eyes of love and compassion, then they will again come to a place of balance. Now Tony knows that the true source of love lies within himself and that by rejecting Ana, he is rejecting himself.

Dealing with Rejection

Abandonment is that sense of rejection that we sometimes feel from others as well as from ourselves, since everything that we create for ourselves in our lives comes from within.

We all experience abandonment and rejection, and the reason for this is that we mistake the real source of love in our lives. We look for love outside ourselves, especially when we are babies or kids. We want our parents to meet absolutely every single need that we have, and we feel that it's our birthright. Sometimes that part of us does not grow to the responsibility of fulfilling our own needs. In a case like that, we often hold a very strong energy of blame towards our parents, our peers, our teachers, our older brothers and sisters. When we do this, though, we are disconnecting ourselves from the true source of love that is within each one of us.

The first wound often occurs when the child's love for the mother is rejected so that it feels that there is something wrong with it because its love is not wanted. As children, we always think it's our fault and that we are the cause of whatever is happening. Especially when we're children, we don't always understand that our parents might be in a place of fear or struggle and that they might have created a wall of protection around themselves. This isolates them from us. We love our parents so we send them love, but because they have created this energy of protection around themselves, we feel that the love that we send bounces back at us and that our love is therefore not wanted. This leads us to feel that *we* are not wanted. We feel rejected and abandoned. We feel that we are doing something wrong and that *we* are wrong, that we are worthless, when in fact we are not responsible for the wall that our parents have created around themselves. That's just the reality of their lives.

So when we go through that experience of having our love rejected, we may react in several different ways. Sometimes we become clingy and needy – the kind of person who is always saying, 'I want love, I need you to listen to me, I want you to do this for me', because we are desperately looking for attention and love. At other times, we may go to the opposite extreme, where we say, 'OK, if my love is not wanted, then you can't have it.' In that case, we isolate ourselves by creating a wall around ourselves – or we play the game of wanting to be chased, where we want the other person to be clingy so that we can then push them away. The point is that when we hold the energy of rejection, it can manifest in different ways.

Now in some relationships, we may be the clingy, needy person, while in others, we may be the one who builds the wall. These two things tend to play themselves out in our lives. One may be more prominent than the other, but both are about searching for love outside ourselves and feeling that sense of rejection when our love is not wanted. When we are being clingy, we experience rejection because the other person wants us to move away. When we create a wall around ourselves, we are also creating rejection because we cannot feel the love that the other person is sending us. That person will then move away from us. So the cycle keeps repeating itself. When we create the energy of rejection, we recreate this cycle over and over and over again. Whether we are rejecting others or whether they are rejecting us doesn't matter. Energetically, there is no difference between rejecting someone and being rejected – it is all the same thing.

As we mature and gain a certain degree of awareness, we realise that the reason our love is not being received might be because there is something else going on with the other person. The other person might be feeling fear or might not want to be loved, or he or she might have some issue and not be ready. So if our love is not being received, it's not necessarily because of us. It's important to move away from labelling ourselves and our love as 'not good enough'. For example, we could try changing to a different label, such as 'maybe the person is not yet ready to receive my love'. This doesn't change who we are, nor does it change our capacity to love and be loved. Sometimes it might even mean that there is a better situation for all involved, and in that case, we are receiving a gift, even if we're not yet ready to acknowledge it as such. Whatever the situation, it is never a measure of our own or the other person's essential worth or character.

Exercise:
Connecting with Rejection

So just take a moment now to connect with your heart and feel its response. What is the first thing that comes to you when asked the following question:

- **How do I feel when my love is rejected?**
  Here are a few options: Alone, isolated, abandoned, angry, unwanted, lost, sad, guilty, shitty, like I'm dying.

Now go back into your heart to connect with your response to the next question:

- **Who do I feel that I am when I am rejected?**
  Again, here are a few possibilities: Addictive, hurt, useless, worthless, scared, incompetent, powerless, victimised, unworthy, like running away, unable to cope, deserving better.

Now try to feel these responses and the sense of identity that they produce in you very clearly. Take a minute to notice what happens with your body, your emotions, your thoughts, your energy as you explore each feeling. Notice any images that arise in your mind and what sorts of feelings these images evoke.

Finding Our Balance

The challenge is for us to be who we really are no matter who we are with. At different times in our lives, we will find ourselves in the presence of people who are closed or open or who project things onto us. How can we be ourselves with those people? It's always a challenge to be still in a busy place. How can we be ourselves and be calm when there is all this noise around us? I always know that I am having a really horrible day when I let the noise affect me. At that point, I say, 'OK, I can feel the anger rising up in me now.' On days like that, I am allowing the environment to trigger different things in me, and sometimes I am grateful because I become aware of something that I need to address.

When we have been hurt, when we create a wall and reject love, it means that there is a power struggle going on. Now you project love towards me, and I reject it because it's my turn to do so and I can play that game, too. It's similar to sending a text message to someone when there is a bit of a conflict going on and then receiving no reply to the text message. You have sent out your power, and the other person is holding the power now. It's the same thing as when we delay communication because we are on a power trip. Now the other person is waiting for a reply.

The ideal situation is to be in a sharing, or flowing, mode. When we withdraw, we are not in the flow of things because we are not accessible. Nothing can flow out of us in that case.

It is not our job to nourish others. The way most of us have been raised is to give, give, give, and if you receive, you are considered selfish with all that goes along with that. But when I am in a place where I can hold love and where I am able to love myself, then I can share love. Sharing love is not the same as giving love – they are two different things. If I have a baby, then I look after the child because it doesn't yet know how to do that for itself. That's something it still needs to learn. In that case, it's a different relationship, and it's not fifty-fifty. In time, the baby grows up and can look after itself, so its diaper does not need to be changed anymore. Somehow, though, we may still feel that we need to help, say, a forty-year-old man. You see this a lot with mothers who sometimes treat us like their little children instead of their bigger adults. The type of nourishing energy that we need as children is very different from the nourishment that we need as adults.

In relationships, it is never about the other person. It's about you being in a place where you feel good about yourself. We need to empower ourselves by learning and growing from the situations and people that we encounter, because if we run away, we will recreate the same situations over and over again. So work through your issues and towards empowerment, and you will attain clarity.

True Source of Love

What is the spiritual wound of rejection and abandonment?

The spiritual wound of rejection occurs when we perceive that our love is not wanted or that the love that we need is not available.

This can take many forms depending on our own experience.

When we mistake the source of love as being in someone else, if that person then rejects us, we feel empty and unloved.

When two people come together and both hold the spiritual wound of rejection, each person will hold one side of the polarity. One will do the rejecting (active), and the other will be rejected (passive).

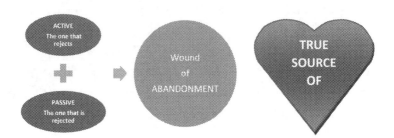

In a case like this, both people have mistaken the real source of love by looking for love in the other person.

So where is the true source of love?

Within YOU!

The only way to heal this wound is to look within and learn to see yourself as the limitless source of love that you are.

THE WOUND OF CONTROL

Unconscious spiritual lesson

- When the wound of Control is active, we attract the person that controls us or the one that we control

Beliefs of control

- He/she is controlling
- I have no power
- Relationships are power struggles
- I can't express myself as I'll be criticised and judged
- I'm the victim, no one loves me
- I'm superior/inferior to you

Feelings of control

- Powerlessness
- Victimisation
- Anger and Resentment

Controlling behaviour

- Exercising authoritative or dominating influence over someone
- Holding someone in restraint
- Submissiveness

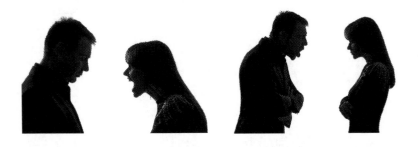

So now the control factor enters in, and what do we see here?

What do you think Tony is thinking and feeling as he is overpowering Ana?

What do you think Ana is feeling as she is being shouted at by Tony?

Think back on your life.

Have you ever been in Tony's position, or have you ever been in Ana's position?

I am sure that we have all been the one pressing down the other person just as I am sure that we have all been the one who has been pressed down. Neither of these positions is free. Both of them carry a sense of powerlessness, so the wound is the same for both of them. One person is overpowering, and the other is overpowered. Even though one is acting actively and the other is acting passively, they are both co-creating the wound of control.

Power Struggle

As we have seen, there is a power struggle taking place here. Both people are seeking power, and they both feel that their power has been misplaced somewhere. Both also need to explore their journey to freedom. So when Tony allows himself to explore the meaning of freedom more deeply, and when both Tony and Ana learn how to manage their own power and know that their power belongs to them as individuals and that it cannot be given away or taken from them, then they will feel safe in being who they are. Then, when Ana finds that space where she feels good enough to be who she is, they will both find that place of balance. Right now, both of them are afraid of losing their power, as they are still in that place where one is active and one is passive rather than both being centred.

When we consciously fall in love with someone, it's because we are attracted to what we see, but unconsciously, our eyes are also seeing the hidden, or shadow, side. So he or she may seem very nice, fun, kind, etc., but unconsciously we are aware that the person is controlling, for example, and will ultimately overpower us. Initially, though, we're not aware of it.

So this is why we come together, and this is why, in an empowered relationship, Ana's wound and Tony's wound is each a great thing if they can both work through their hurt in such a way that they learn to know themselves better. That's how an empowered relationship works. Some people's view of relationships is of couples drinking martinis on the beach all day ... sorry, but that's not real. A really good relationship is when a person is able to act out some pain or wound and you can really be there for them.

Different Forms of Control

For some reason, we want to control our relationships. This means that we develop a resistance to suffering because none of us really wants to suffer. But in trying to control suffering, we only create more suffering.

There is a part of us that is the controlling person, and there is a part of us that is the controlled. We experience this as an inner struggle. We all have that part of us that feels that his or her freedom is being taken away, and we also all have that part of us that takes away our own freedom. At the end of the day, freedom cannot be given to us nor can it be taken away from us. Freedom is who we are – it is the essence of our soul.

So when you are in a situation where you are the controller or the bully, that means that there is an inner power struggle and that there is a part of you that is not allowing you to be free. In the same way, if you feel that you are being controlled from outside yourself, that also means that the inner controller has taken over the part of you that is being controlled. This is how your freedom is controlled, because the only person who can take control away from you is you.

The questions we first need to ask ourselves are:

1. **How do we control people through our minds?**
   Active mental control means trying to make people think the same way we think, and we can find different

ways to try to do this. Even passive mental control can influence someone to change their way of thinking.

2. **How do we control people through our emotions?**
Emotional control also occurs in both its active and passive forms. When our hearts are too open or too closed, that means there is an emotional control issue. Emotional control can be hard to pinpoint through observation alone, because its real influence on others is not always obvious. The super nice way some people have of telling others that they look great when the comment doesn't come from a sincere place is an example of this type of attempt to control.

3. **How do we control people through our bodies?**
Bodily control takes a variety of forms. For example, if I want something done my way, I might stand up and say, 'OK, we are doing this.' Someone else in that case might feel uncomfortable or threatened by my body language. It can have a similar effect as someone saying, 'If you don't do what I want, I'll punch you.'
Other ways we gain control are with sexual energy and even with what seems to be the opposite of aggression, as when someone smiles to get their own way with a person or situation. Whether we are attempting to gain control or whether we are being controlled, with many aspects of that energy, there is a wound and there is pain because the energy of who we really are is freedom. We forget that we are the energy of freedom and that when someone controls us, it is because we are giving our freedom away. We can also get confused and think

that we need to control others in order to be free, but this is a false sense of freedom with no basis in reality.

Healing Control

Two people co-create a struggle when one person wants something that the other person doesn't want to give.

We shouldn't deliberately look for confrontation because we feel we need to learn from the experience, but when confrontation arises, we should stop and say, 'OK, I have an opportunity here to use my freedom, so I choose not to react but to be calm. I choose to be in the energy of struggle, but I won't allow myself to be a part of the struggle, and I won't allow the struggle to control me, to bring me down or to make me feel aggressive. I will be in this energy without judging it – just observing it. I will just be. If you can remain calm when you become involved in a struggle, then there can be more understanding between you and the other person. Your goal should be to be calm, no matter what. If you can do this, then the next time something happens, you will be able to stay free.

Remove the word **CONFRONTATION** from your vocabulary, and replace it with **NEGOTIATION**!

Don't judge yourself when you are doing everything you can and you cannot be calm. There are things that we are not at ease with, but very often they will kick-start the journey for us.

For example, you would not punish a two-year old because he can't drive a car. You accept that he doesn't yet have the life experience to be able to drive a car. In the same way, we need to allow ourselves the freedom to learn and grow and make choices. There are no mistakes. So let's just learn with awareness, which means being aware of everything that happens in our lives.

Freedom

What Is the Spiritual Wound of Control?

The spiritual wound of control has to do with the misuse of power.

We identify it when we perceive that power is being taken away from us or when we feel a need to overpower the other person.

When two people come together and play out this wound, one will control (active) and the other will feel controlled (passive).

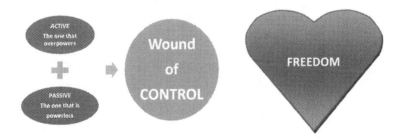

In essence, both people are searching for freedom. But freedom cannot be given to you nor can it be taken away from you, since you are FREEDOM.

THE WOUND OF FEAR

Unconscious spiritual lesson

- When the wound of Fear is active, we attract the person that distrusts us or the one that we distrust

Beliefs of fear

- I don't trust her/him
- Don't listen to your heart – listen to your head
- Don't let anyone too close
- Everyone is trying to hurt me
- I'm not safe; it's not safe to love or be loved

Feelings of fear

- Anxiety
- Panic
- Distrust
- Suspicion
- Being uneasy or apprehensive

Fear behaviour

• Questioning your partner's motives

Tony steps away from Ana.

Tony is feeling fear and distrust in himself, in others, and in his relationship. Now Ana senses this fear and does not know what's going on with this dynamic.

What do you think Tony is thinking and feeling as he experiences fear and distrust towards Ana?

What do you think Ana is feeling as she is being distrusted?

Think back on your life.

Have you ever been in Tony's position, or have you ever been in Ana's position?

She moves closer, and he gets more scared. Tony needs more space, so Ana moves back. In an empowered relationship, Tony would be willing to learn about trust. But it's not so much about trusting Ana as about trusting himself, and Ana needs to learn to trust herself also. If she stands still and holds the energy of trust, then this can help Tony to feel more comfortable around her.

This brings us back to the issue of trust and that we don't trust ourselves enough to be loved – and especially that we don't trust ourselves with Unconditional Love because we don't know what that is. I would dare to say that very few of us have experienced Unconditional Love. We have all experienced love on many levels, and sometimes we experience the 'Wow! love factor, and we think that that is it. But the truth is that there is a lot more.

Staying Centred

We sometimes need to first learn what not to do in order to learn what to do. As we explored earlier, we perceive things as good and bad, but this perception is not true on a spiritual level. True perception is about accepting everything and knowing that everything has a purpose.

Here is a scenario that illustrates this sort of dynamic. Let's say I am in love with a wonderful man and he gives me a bouquet of flowers. Naturally, I am thrilled with the flowers and that he loves me so much. But then he forgets my birthday, and I am devastated.

Now if I can remain centred in that place where there is no projection, then if the man gives me flowers, I simply think of it as a lovely gesture. And when I experience the fact that he forgets my birthday, I just accept that wherever he is right now in his life is the reason he forgot in the first place. So in both instances, I am in a place of acceptance that brings me neither happiness nor sadness. Obviously, the different actions have different effects, but in both cases I remain calm and centred and accept both realities. The important thing is that I don't allow the unconscious drama to take over.

Staying Present

The main point to take away when dealing with fear is that it sabotages our relationships, but the way to deal with this is to allow our whole being to be present. We can only create when we are present – we cannot create when we are absent. To be present with our sense of fear and distrust is to allow trust to take place and to become integrated. Then we are present with our partners and we can co-create. One step at a time can make this happen, and since we move in layers, it will take time, as many other influences tend to come in.

Identifying Gender-Related Fears

So what are the aspects of male and female energies that most scare us? What is our biggest fear in relation to the duality of gender? As a woman, what is your fear? As a man, what is your fear?

The following examples can pertain to either gender:

- Examples of fears expressed by women
  Being alone
  Getting hurt
  Being abused
  Being old
  Making mistakes
  Not learning

- Examples of fears expressed by men
  Male aggression
  Overly controlling females
  Inability to express emotions

Let's take a look at the power struggle between men and women in the world at the moment. What do we feel that men and women want from this power struggle?

- Women would like men to be less egotistical, less concerned with money, power, control.
- Men would like to think that women won't try to change them.
- It's still a very male-dominated world. Women would like genuine equality between male and female.
- Women are at fault as much as men. Men would like women to shoulder some of the blame and responsibility for the present condition of things.
- There's still the frame of mind with some generations that women should stay at home while men go to work. There is a growing feeling among both men and women that they would like to see some loosening of traditional gender-role expectations.
- Women like to express qualities such as sensuality, compassion, and charity; but they feel that, because of this, they're not given an equal chance in life.
- Men and women hold the same jobs but get different salaries. Women would like equal pay for equal work and job type.
- Sometimes women have to act like men at their jobs because of the feeling that companies don't like feminine energy. Women would like to be acknowledged as equals and valued for themselves without having to adjust their characters to suit a male-dominated world.
- There is a growing number of men who would like to spend more time with their kids while they are

still babies. This shows that, like women, men are also looking for a fuller expression and experience in life.

- This generation of men talks more about feelings than past generations. Men would like to be acknowledged for having progressed in the area of emotional honesty and awareness.

- We are creating change for ourselves for the better and passing it on to our young children. Both men and women would like to look forward to better lives and relationships for themselves and their children.

The power struggle that is going on in the world is no different from the power struggle that is going on within us. If we are still getting angry about what's happening on the outside, that means that we are holding that energy within ourselves.

Trust

What is the spiritual wound of fear?

The spiritual wound of fear occurs when we distrust the flow of life, when we distrust ourselves.

When two people come together and play out this wound, one distrusts (active), and the other feels distrusted (passive).

The wound of fear means that both people are looking for trust outside themselves. But trust only happens within.

THE WOUND OF SEPARATION

Unconscious spiritual lesson

- When the wound of Separation is active, we attract the person that withdraws from us or the one that we withdraw from

Beliefs of separation

- My thoughts and feelings are not to be shared
- I need space
- Relationships are clingy and suffocating
- I can't express myself as I'll be criticised and judged
- I'm disconnected from everyone

Feelings of separation

- Disconnection
- Suffocation
- Clinginess

- Isolation
- Brokenness

Separation behaviour

- The state of lacking unity
- Lack of connection or continuity
- The act of secluding yourself from others

Tony disconnects from Ana physically and emotionally and has become completely separated from Ana.

What do you think Tony is thinking and feeling as he withdraws from Ana?

What do you think Ana is feeling as she is isolated?

Think back on your life.

Have you ever been in Tony's position, or have you ever been in Ana's position?

What would happen if Ana tried to reach him?

As she moves in, he moves further away.

In an empowered relationship, to heal separation and bring about union, Tony will need to open up and allow himself to connect with Ana.

When we separate, we disconnect. When we are in that lovely honeymoon period, everything is great, and then suddenly one person disconnects and the other is left wondering, 'Oooohhh, what's going on here?' That person then moves in closer and smothers the other with his or her needs. So Tony needs to find out and know that union happens within him, and Ana needs to find out the same thing.

Losing Sight of Ourselves

At those times in our lives when we are exploring the experience of separation and when that is absolutely our reality, we see every occurrence through the eyes of separation. We are forever looking outward for the things that seem to be missing in our lives. Our sense of separation from ourselves brings us great pain that we then recreate over and over again in our lives.

From the moment we enter into this world, we experience separation from our source. The next separation is from our mothers at birth. Then there is our first day at school, eventually followed by the separation that occurs when we leave our families. Other examples include relationship break-ups, the death of a close friend or relative, and so on. I feel that the main emotion of separation is loss. We are even afraid of losing ourselves, and this creates either conflict, such as an argument, or a situation where fear kicks in.

So what does it mean to lose ourselves, and what is the fear that we experience around losing ourselves? How do we experience that sense of loss? How do we feel in a relationship or friendship or job situation where we've lost the sense of who we are?

The fear that a lot of us have in our relationships is that if we give too much, we will lose ourselves in the situation. We need to understand, though, that losing ourselves is a perception that is not real. It is great to be independent of a partner, but it's also good to understand that the life we create together with a partner can be as involved or as uninvolved as we want it to be. The relationship between our mutual energies can come in many sizes, and even though we are creating with another person, our individual independence will never be lost.

We have all experienced the feeling of losing ourselves. I was in a relationship where I completely lost myself, and it took me two years to get back to a place where I knew who I was. I lost myself because I disempowered myself – because I put the other person first so much that I didn't matter at all. In the process, I ended up losing my sense of self, and I then had to take the very painful journey of learning not to lose myself again.

So this is the process that we go through. Above all, the fear of losing ourselves comes from the fact that we don't trust ourselves and that we don't know who we really are. Who we are is the essence of love, the essence of freedom, of power, and of peace. That is who we really are, and that can never be lost because it's our essential nature. I feel that when we lose ourselves that what is really happening is that we are becoming invisible to ourselves. I feel that when we cannot see ourselves, that's when the fear of losing ourselves takes over.

This inability to see ourselves completely can happen for different reasons. For example, I was once involved in a relationship that caused me to completely neglect my friends so that the part of myself that I once knew disappeared and went over to the unseen part. I used to be outgoing and spontaneous, but because of this relationship, I became sad and depressed and didn't want to socialise. Then all of a sudden the relationship ended, but I found that I could no longer see the part of myself that I once could see because I had lost all connection with it. It had become a part of my invisible side. The truth is that nothing had been lost, but I now had to go on a journey through the unseen to get back to what I once was able to see. For two years, I worked on finding my way out of this situation, and during that time I could not communicate with anyone as there were no words to express what I was feeling and experiencing. I realised that I needed to lose myself in order to find myself, and when I finally did find myself, I vowed never to lose myself again. This vow did not come from a place of fear but from a place of empowerment, because I realised what I had done to myself. The process of bringing those parts of myself out of hiding to where I could see them once again was hard work, and once I got them back, I said to myself, 'This is staying here'.

So when we lose ourselves, what's really happening is that we are becoming invisible to ourselves. It is our job then to make ourselves visible. When we are in that place of 'Oh, I only love the ten percent of myself that I can handle', that is when we create that sense of loss because we are not embracing ourselves one hundred percent. Of course, this is all a process since we all need to realise that we have the ability to be open to one hundred percent pure love, but it has to start with ourselves.

Union

What is the spiritual wound of separation?

The spiritual wound of separation occurs when we perceive ourselves as disconnected from ourselves and others.

When two people come together and play out this wound, there are feelings of being alone and isolated. One person withdraws (active), and the other becomes clingy and suffocating (passive).

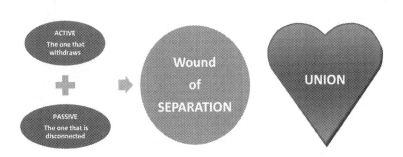

The wound of separation means that both people are looking for UNION outside themselves. When we connect with all aspects of ourselves, we realize that UNION happens within and that, in truth, we were never separate.

THE MESSAGES WE LEARN FROM OUR WOUNDS

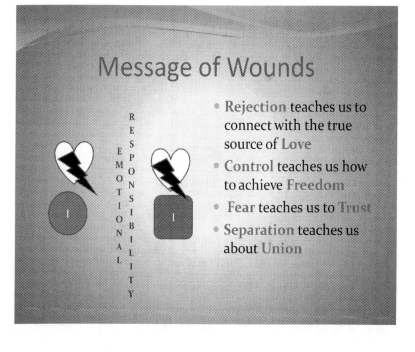

Our Wounds are our greatest teachers, it's through them that we learn emotional responsibility so that we can love without any limitations.

- **Rejection teaches us to connect with the true source of Love**
- **Control teaches us how to achieve Freedom**
- **Fear teaches us to Trust**
- **Separation teaches us about Union**

HOW TO CREATE EMPOWERED RELATIONSHIPS ...

1. **Accept Their Uniqueness.** Learn to love and appreciate the way your partner shows love. Don't expect everyone to show love the same way that you do.
2. **Shift Your Focus.** Notice what your partner is doing for you instead of focusing on what he or she is not doing.
3. **Create Empowered Communication.** Move away from blame, and realize that all situations have been created by both individuals.
4. **Allow for Personal Healing.** The more you love and accept yourself, the more you'll be able to create a loving relationship.
5. **Become Love.** As we explore the polarities of giving and receiving love, we come to embody LOVE. Learn to love yourself through your partner.
6. **Establish Boundaries.** Learn to create empowered physical, emotional, mental and spiritual boundaries.

7. **Be Aware.** Become aware of the major wounds played out in the relationship and replace them with higher truths:

Abandonment/True Source of Love

Separation/Connection

Fear/Trust

Control/Freedom

8. **Stay Present.** Work at clearing energetic imprints or unresolved issues or traumas from previous relationships.
9. **Commit to Love.** Allow yourself to stay in the relationship when the Inner Saboteur wants to run away.
10. **Nurture Sacred Sexuality.** Allow a deeper connection.

When we accept another's love, we are loving ourselves.

Can we ever be pain-free?

Only when we accept that our human experience, sadness, loneliness, separation, and so on are not the root cause of pain but the way that individuals choose to express their disconnection with themselves.

Every single moment
LIFE is bringing you
the opportunity
to LOVE yourself
MORE!

ABOUT THE AUTHOR

I started training as a holistic therapist in 1997. My own journey started exploring different Energy Therapies.

- **Shamanic Practitioner**
- **Reiki Master**
- **Integrated Energy Therapy Master-Instructor**
- **Magnified Healing Teacher**
- **Theta Healing Practitioner**
- **Bach Flower Dance Teacher**

Once I got full understanding of energy I felt the need to understand the body so I studied different types of massage. I trained in Thailand at ITM massage school in Chiang Mai:

- **Teaching Diploma in Thai Massage**
- **Thai Foot Reflexology**
- **Oil massage**
- **Thai Herbal Massage**
- **Body and Facial Treatments**
- **Hopi Ear Candles**

After understanding the relationship between energy and body I felt the need to understand the mind, I studied Psychotherapy.

And after that I felt I could really offer a holistic approach to my clients. Mind, Body and Soul.

- Diploma and Advanced Diploma in Clinical Hypnotherapy - Psychotherapy
- Understanding and Helping Survivors of Sexual Abuse and Rape
- Couple Attachment & Marital fit
- <u>CBT (Cognitive Behavioral Therapy)</u>
- <u>Life Coaching</u>
- <u>Breakthrough Parenting Instructor</u>
- Currently studying a 2 year diploma in Jungian studies

For 1 to 1 sessions or more information go to: www.empowered-relationships.com

Printed in the United States
By Bookmasters